Sandy ~~Heard~~ - Rm. 230 -
9/18

Murray Dre...
speaker...
subject: ...

Form...
Life after Traumatic
Brain Injury

PROOF

PROOF

Poems by Murray Dunlap

For Ashley, Connor, William, Sam, & Bennet

Stick with it!

The Country Bookshop

Boomer Press

Southern Pines, North Carolina

The Country Bookshop
140 NW Broad Street
Southern Pines, North Carolina 28387

Printed in the United States of America
First published as a Boomer Press paperback

Book Design by Judi Hewett

Author Photo by Jaymie Baxley

ISBN 978-0-999131-71-8

Yes, I survived the impossible.

But no, I did not do it alone.

With God's grace and the unstoppable love of my wife,

I have created a rewarding life from one

that had burned to the ground.

Thank you, Mary Balfour, for your beautiful heart.

This book is for you.

Introduction

I've known Murray Dunlap since he and I were boys, so don't expect an unbiased introduction here. We both grew up in Mobile, AL, and his mother and my mother have been great friends for longer than I can remember and his older brother, DR, and I became great friends in our teens. Murray was just enough years younger that his is a more peripheral presence in my memory—an aspiring painter, a cross country star at our high school, someone whose path I intersected with now and then as DR and I got up to whatever kind of trouble we were getting up to in those days. Maybe he was already writing poems and stories back then but the truth is, I can't recall.

It was only later, when Murray moved to Charlottesville, Virginia, that he and I really got to know each other, that he became my friend and not my friend's little brother. He was about to begin an MA in creative writing at UC Davis and was trying to get his stories published and I'd just finished a stint as a visiting writer at Hollins College and returned to Charlottesville where my new wife was working and where I'd done my MFA. We'd get together now and then to go fly-fishing. We'd swap manuscripts and talk about books. I discovered in

Murray a kindred spirit, a person with the same complicated connection to the place of our birth and the people who raised us, a person ready to dedicate his life to telling stories.

It's strange to think, as I write these words, that the young man in my memory no longer exists. Not really, not exactly. That "young man died," Murray writes in *Proof*, "and I wear his mask." He is referring, of course, to his accident and the coma and amnesia that followed and his subsequent recovery and ultimately, the beginning of a new existence. "I am Murray Dunlap," he writes. "I am not Murray Dunlap."

I have seen many of the changes wrought in Murray, the way the accident shattered his body and the way he battled to be whole again, the way his rage at being broken morphed into a kind of peace and abiding faith and a new way of understanding what it means to be alive. But those lines in particular sent me back to his first book, *Bastard Blue*, a collection of linked stories written before the accident that changed his life. I guess I was curious to see if the paradox—"I am Murray Dunlap/I am not Murray Dunlap"—held true of his writing as well.

Honestly, I was surprised by how much *Bastard Blue* and *Proof* have in common. Both share concision of language. Both are rich in love and dogs. Both are shot through with anger and frustration and no small measure of regret. Both are leavened with hope. Both are worthy of our best attention. When reading these two books side by side, however, I couldn't shake the feeling that they were written by two distinctly different human beings.

I have been trying to put my finger on the source of this feeling for some time now and I have been aware, for the last couple of sentences, that I was writing toward the moment when I would be obliged to elaborate, but now that I'm here, I find myself at a loss for words. Or perhaps what I want to say is too complicated for words. Let's try this: Every writer worth reading has his own unique way of looking at the world. That's what's changed in Murray, I think, and it is impossible for anyone except the man himself to render true. It is related to the marvel of his recovery and to the family that supported him on his journey from one Murray Dunlap to the next and to the fact that he was granted another chance at real and everlasting love and to faith, bred into him by all these miracles, and to the inner strength that carried him through his most brutal hours and carries him onward still. Thank God that you have his words instead of mine to distinguish the man he has become, to let you live inside of his experience.

An element of every writer's way of looking at the world is memory—of place and people and experience, good and bad—but Murray's accident robbed him of significant swaths of his. He touches on his amnesia in *Proof*. "Tiny spots of memory/ Collectively make no sense." Memory is, one the other hand, the least precise of our mental functions, so bear with me for the rest of this introduction.

I don't recall with absolute certainty if I heard the following from DR or if Murray's mother told my mother and she passed it on to me or if Murray told me himself. I choose to remember the more personal and direct exchange. That's another reason memory is so close the writer's process. There's an undeniable element of creativity in remembering.

What I'm trying to tell you is that some months after Murray woke up from his coma, we spent an afternoon together in Mobile. I asked too many questions and he answered them as best he could and one of the things that emerged in our conversation is that out of all the memories stolen from him in the accident, he remembered that he was a writer, as if being a writer is fundamental to his nature, some un-erasable part of himself. That notion takes my breath away. It also speaks to the paradox raised in *Proof.* "I am Murray Dunlap/ I am not Murray Dunlap." Murray Dunlap, the writer, lived through his accident and woke up from that coma and wrote the book that you are holding in your hands and what a blessing that is for all of us, what a blessing to bear witness as he makes his memories and his life and the man himself anew.

— Michael Knight, author and essayist

Table of Contents

Table of Contents

"And I wanna have friends that I can trust,
that love me for the man I've become, not the man I was."

— THE AVETT BROTHERS

PROOF

Proof (for VW)

The wreck was unspeakable
My injuries, severe
The fact that I smile
Is proof

No. I did not walk away
No. I was carried
But breathing, yes
My heartbeat, strong
Out of wreckage
I am born again

I live and I write
As proof of a perfect safety
Unthinkable survival
My heart cradled inside
My life, balanced in airbags and steel
Proven solid, proven smiles

The proof: I am alive

Writer in Residence

I am here at Weymouth
In theory, to write.
I am here to answer questions
To those who stop by
No one does

I consume the silence
Polish my poems
I edit in earnest
I write this poem, but little else is new
I polish and polish my story
I hope to shine

Proof that I did, in fact, survive
Proof that I will continue the journey
Proof that I married well
Proof that I believe
That I live and love and laugh and cry

I have Proof
It is in your hands right now

If the World Was Fair

If the world was fair
There would be no accidents
No thieves
No lies
Doctors could cure every last thing
If the world was fair
We would love everyone we met
There would be no hate

But the world is not fair
Red lights are run
Some wives only want money
Therapy does not always work
Doctors do not have every answer

And if God made a perfect world
What would we learn
How would we be grateful
What would we know at all?

Amnesia

Tiny spots of memory
Collectively make no sense
An image begins to form
And suddenly all is lost
The ugly truth of the big picture
The trials of trying to remember
Fail Fail Fail
Amnesia

The Art of Art

In the finer times of life
We are driven to reflect our smiles
In the worst of times
We moan hardship
Both are driving to explain our hearts
Explanation through art
Sight, sound, and word
A tender melody may give soundtrack
For painting and typing
The art of art has found me

A Thoughtful Response

Quick answers are not planned
Not as rich as one wants
But with the time needed
We give back so much more
One man asks his girl
Do you love me?
She reflects, breathes deeply, and raises an eyebrow
Then, exhaling, she responds with a smile
The air between them froze
Complicated relationships
Deserve more
But often we find answers in the curl of a lip
The angle of an eyebrow
The chisel of a chin
The finer movements in our face
Often speak without words

Mask of Truth

The young man died
And I wear his mask
In sadness I tell his friends to move along
That young man no longer lives here
He no longer writes anything you might remember
He no longer has the right skills for a crowd
He gives readings in an attempt to make a new life
A new man
I wear his mask, but I cannot act right
I cannot think right
I cannot be that man
Instead, I wear a mask of truth
A cowering memory
Of that young man who died
I am Murray Dunlap
I am not Murray Dunlap

The Light of Her Eyes, The Light of His

I married a priest
An exceptional fact
I was lost, confused, and angry
But the light in her eyes
Told me not to give up
Not to cry
The light of His eyes
Came out of hers
The eyes of life
Forgave my anger
Lit me right up
And made me smile

Eyes of Gold

A beautiful friend
With liver cancer, no doubt
Owen wags his tail as he limps
To the very end -pain be damned
With eyes of gold, Owen stands by us
Fetch? Not even when he was healthy
Comfort a friend? Owen is our best friend on earth
Bark a squirrel away, give our neighbors a
sarcastic growl
Not in my yard, not on my watch
You give us your best, Owen
We love you
And after you have gone
We will love you all the more

Love Steps In

Indeed, we walk
Among the leaves, betwixt the winds
Howling indelicate words
We are heavy-laden to speak of finance
Money moves us, indeed
And yet we do not allow it into our polite conversation
Who has what? And what do they use it for?
For good? For evil? Maybe just self-indulgence... this one time
Leaves filter down, around our feet
We watch our step
And we laugh when appropriate piles collect
Draw up a stem for closer inspection, deciding value
An ugly occupation that finds us all
Intimidating, to say the least
Value carries power
Power carries respect
In diamonds, we even value love --how dare us?
Perhaps we should appraise our hearts
Giving them the final say
And love steps in

My Time

Coma close
But it wasn't my time
Wheelchair walks
But it wasn't my time
Marital madness
But it wasn't my time
Dating demon
But it wasn't my time
I roll up my sleeves
And the gloves are off
In my time
I narrow my eyes
And furrow my brow
In my time
Defying the impossible
But I'll let God decide
When my time is up

Grace

With the taste of wine still on my tongue, I have
come to the realization that I now truly understand
what the word grace means.
In our service, as always, there were words. This time,
I honestly listened. And there is grace.
I wanted to be a writer. Now I am one.
And there is grace.
My beautiful forever-wife has a beautiful heart.
And there is grace.
I was truly afraid. Now I am truly happy.
And there is grace.
I was weak. Now I am strong.
And there is grace.
Our amazing family helped us move here.
We love them. And there is grace.
I was confused and lost. Now I am found.
And there is grace.
The lighting at Emmanuel cast the most vivid glow
on the faces of many people who we will instantly
love. And there is grace.
I have been through it. I fought my way back.
And there is grace.

Brain Injury

At the front door
You will come and go
The rug, well worn
Your presence, felt
Ornamental sculptures in the sideboard
A painting at its crown
Speak here in traditional language
Shake hands and hug

The lawn slopes down in the back
Basement window, hidden
Some claw through
Not invited, they climb
On dirty elbows and knees
We do not speak here
We do not shake hands or hug
Nothing ornamental
In this removed place

Communicate in sign language
To those already here
We sit in silence
Our wounds, unseen

We tap out S...O...S...
In the hope we are found
While the sounds of a party
Echo down the stairs

We hear laughter
And social sounds
Clinking glasses
Shuffling feet

Surely someone knows we are here
Someone might speak our tongue
And translate our pain?

The Time of My Life

An intrepid traveler
I hitchhiked through coma
I hiked past wheelchair
Insanity struck as lightning
Shifting gears, I drove to love and happiness
I ran to God
I could not find my way until I met Him
We caught up in mother's garage
Balanced between hate, fear, and forgiveness
He told me to slow down
Recovery is not a race
I finally interpret Him in ways that make sense
Allowing me to reach my destination
True love and thoughtful waking hours
I smile straight, knowing...
This is the time of my life

Hairstreaks and Blues

Grass and goldenrod weaving knots, thick and blight
Seen through cracked panes, frames to rot
Fish crow talons tight and the black wire slope
Dog-day cicadas click and hum

Restless in linen sheets, curled in twist, fold, and
crumble
Scratching and rustling, mantis legs fold forward

And the scent of your hair, braided into the fabric
Caught and hung like an old robe, silent behind the
maple door
Propped with shadow, contoured with quivering light

Thin drafts dance across the floor
Pastoral ants collect from hairstreaks and blues
Honeydew

Bedding with memories
Prayers of a mantis
And the scent of your hair, braided into fabric

Long Days

The day is long
And I am weary
Apologies go nowhere
Not well received
I am anxious to love
And have it returned
The day is longer than I can handle
But the anxiety
Is earned
I am sorry to so many
I hate my mistakes
What has passed, has passed
One wonders who can forgive me
I wonder if I am whole

Defining Marriage

Her eyes when your favorite person smiles
Her eyes that say: Yes, ok, let's do this
The same eyes as when she said yes

The finest breath you take
The deepest, lung-filling air that means:
This is forever, don't screw this up
Not now, not ever

That look in her eye when you have done
  something wrong
That look of her trying to see how it might be right
That look of forgiveness, when it is not

The nuances of love
Now that you can see straight
Now that you can think, and breathe
The truth of love, the forever truth
That your best friend is for life
Marriage

The Light Shines On

Like a candle lit for peace
Like the embrace of a dear friend
The warm glow of light
Of feelings touching the soul
Will sustain us
Through dark days
Through dark nights
The earthly hardship
Pain around us
Daggers of betrayal
But the light shines on
The glow warms us each
Restores our faith
The light in our eyes
And on our tongue
Inside our depths
Help us Lord
Shine on, shine on

Reward

The song of calm
A mask of relative ease
Unearned peace does not reward
I carve words
I filter meaning
A new man
A new life
Flashing silver
Dances above
In times of struggle
I cry for a new world
I cry for a world that has gone
Vanishing safety
I am certain of two things
Let go of that easy past
And work for more
Do not dwell
Work
The world is hard
We strive

Hey God, Thanks for Coming

Behind boat motor blades
I am pulled in to safety
Hey God, thanks for coming

On the precipice of a grand mountain
I clip in, safe
Hey God, thanks for coming

Singing tires to crushed metal
Airlifted home
Hey God, thanks for coming

Blood in my eyes, flat on my back
I drive to safety
Hey God, thanks for coming

With unfocused eyes, I fall into traffic
Brakes lock down
Hey God, thanks for coming

I summon the courage to ask
And an angel says, 'I do'
Hey God, thanks for coming

The Damselfish of Hope

Life is a glorious party
Jacquard invitations mailed
Hey God, thanks for coming
The Damselfish of Hope

A fish, new in these shallows
Darts around a black stone
An outcropping of pain
The Damselfish of Hope

The time to heal
Eases into saltwater swells
The need for hope
Swims in as faith

The Damselfish, scales as velvet
A white collar at her neck
Swimming smoothly to safety
Brings you along

Blessings of the Damselfish of Hope

Fever

In the heat of fever
The mind spins, careless
Sweat announces the condition, and starry eyes
Slowed response
Delirium, delirium

Elegant eyes
Uplifted chin
A smoldering glance, hot
Heat of another nature, gives us fever
The fever of passion
On silken sheets, we burn

Intrinsic thought
Basic needs
We survive by care
We evolve by love

Eloquent Insanity

Lies and broken bones
Truth and a broken brain
Where do I begin?

Desire for reimbursement
Desire for identity
Dime a dozen mask
Who am I?

Fallen dreams
Fallen strategies
Rise to love
Step into sanity

Not even close

If I Were the Devil

I married a priest
I attend church, every time
I am a good Christian

But the thoughts do still come
At night, with fear
Thoughts of my ex, my wretched ex
She claimed that I raped her
She claimed that I lied
She wanted dollars; she needed sense

If I were the Devil, I'd take her to hell
No questioning, no wonder
Ripped from this earth
I'd pull her to rot

Fear and loathing bring forth my demons
Bring out the Devil in me
If I were the Devil, I'd waste no time
Instead, I'd focus on torture and pain
If I were the Devil, I'd rip her to hell

But I am not
I am a good Christian
But the thoughts do still come
Never shaking them
I'll fight fear with my thoughts
Of the Devil in me

Fighting

At times, we struggle
Heads above water, then not
Waves submerge our stoicism
Lucifer laughs

At times, we fight
Our best offense
Down on our knees
Our heart, our faith

The thunder of love
Buoys our hearts
Fills our minds with hope
With hope and love

Until we cease fighting
Our temporary death, only a pause
We are each reborn
We each resume the struggle
Our endless loop

Showboat Blues

A brain injury symptom
Announce your success
Big things:
I can walk!
Little things:
I wrote a poem!
Mixed results
Embarrassment
When it all shakes out
I wish I had shut up

Elegant Keys

There are elegant keys
Waiting for our girls
They learn to play
Learn to sing
Among the countless endeavors
They will play
The elegant keys
Paid for by Papa
A grandfather smiles
The tunes and the voices
Perfectly in key

Christ Episcopal Church, Fairfield

Amidst the employees
My wife is a priest
And at Christ Church
We are welcomed
In an unsavory part of town
On the rebound
Corey's Kitchen opens their doors
Pulls out a chair
And serves up the finest meal I have devoured
In eight long years
The courses, well timed
Well spaced
The food, so very delightful
Such perfect temperature
Such perfect portion and spice
Our God-given meal, perfect

Eyes of Art

When my arms ache
And the brain knots
I see files of information leaking away
Impossible to keep things in any proper order
I reach for a brush
The canvas greets me and things make sense
While filing is black and white
I unwind in color
With the eyes of art
We see true

A Severe Life

Glasgow Coma Scale: 13 or above, mild
9 to 12: moderate
8 or below: severe
They watch the eyes
Stimulation
They wait for response
I was a 6
We knew the odds
But the odds did not know me
Severity be damned
Write a book
Marry a priest
Live life
Happiness: severe

Now

Immediately
I light myself on fire
I am ready
For a bigger life
For the world to know
I am alive
Right now

Light

Anger consumes me
And my nonsense life
I'll strive externally
For the definition of light
Meaning evades me
Answers take flight
Depression is darkness
Instead I rely on
The warmth of light
Confusion leads me
To my meaningless plight
I'll bask, instead, in the truth of light

Fellowship of the Sun

The lake of purity draws us in
For an evening among friends
We toast and swim
And then steer the boat
To dine as the sun falls to the horizon
And creates a spectacular view
We relay jokes and tales
Amid children's laughter
And we feel, at last, that we belong
Our fellowship of the sun

The Words We Cower To

Inflammatory defamation
Seditious howls
A fiery burn
But my father
Stands in shadow
His tempered tone
His calm
Never rose his voice
Never howled at me
Not once did he cry out
Rather, with paced selectivity
His words chosen carefully
"Son," he slowly offered
"You do not belong"

To Love Another

To love another
Takes work
To understand needs and wants
And put those ahead of your own
To love another
Is grace
To love another
Is God lending a hand
I love another
With the grace of God
And I think she loves me

In a world of hurt
There is goodness just the same
Goodness and love
As long as there is another

Boats Are in My Blood

Boats are in my blood
A rising tide drifts in
Pulling me toward it
Shipbuilding gave our start
Motors propelled the family
Then the war led us astray
But a Sunfish brought us home
Easing in soundless
Boats are in my blood

In Another Life

I might understand
In another life
Why the pain was allowed
Needed
Deserved
So very intense

And why I pushed through
Despite it
Angry with it
Tested by it
Quivering from it
Succumbing to it

But it ended with love
That may be
All the answer I need

Within the Words

Within the words
We live and breathe and define our presence
Within the words
Our lives are explained
And we are remembered
Within the words
A timeless epiphany
A black on white valued announcement
Within the words
I create myself
I make myself a better man
The illusory moments of life
Entwined in ink on paper
Within the words
I exist

Hallowed

I rise to walk
Not roll
And I forgive
My interruption
This ground is hallowed

In an Instant

He glances side to side
Cars accelerate into other lanes,
  headed who knows where
Birds collect insects from between blades of grass
Gold squirms

In one gulp, a Bluejay turns an ant into a snack
There are no for-sale signs where he had been told
  they would be
In the swallow of a Bluejay, the light turns red
He does not see it

And in an instant
A long distance runner is put in a wheelchair
But three months of coma first
And a divorce, a medicated agony
Goes final

In one gulp
A Bluejay turns lunch into a decade of eating
A mile becomes a thousand
A marriage turns to dust

In an instant, the world goes still
And gray
And turns a lighter shade of blue
A pale comparison to all forward movement
All trials end with a gavel swing
And in an instant, he forgets how to love

Lights

Before the peering window
She sits with ivory hairbrush
Drawing hair out, straight down
The lights in her eyes change
From glow to caution
The stoplight goes red

Her preening had announced warmth
A readiness to dance
But eyes flicker red
Suddenly a threat
High beams fill the room
Her nudity revealed
Then killed with silken robes

Varnished thoughts
Tawdry temptations

Light changes everything

Another Day

In another day or two
We cling to our memories
Of what is happening right now
I want to remember
I want to be sure
Our memories of love and happiness
Guide us out of depression
Guide us out of sadness and gloom
We remember the laughter
We remember the smiles
With amnesia, I forget
And fight to keep my wherewithal
And pray for happiness
In a dark world
I heal like a rising sun
The flames of love
Light me up
I remember that, and thank God

Trapped in Glass

The ease of lofty plans
The melody of a lullaby
Cutting a sail to sleep
Obvious incompletion of sanity
Quiet tremors in a world gone mad

Thoughts cut like wire
In the palm of your hand
The daylight brings divinity
And the moon cloaks a fool

A scene of chaos
Floating waves of doubt
Emulate a faster pattern
The idea of genius
Trapped in glass
And quiet tremors in a world gone mad

Foreigner

I am a foreigner in this strange place
Déjà vu, but nothing returns
An entirely new life I will make
In a new eminence

My silence can be understood
By my lack of understanding
But speak, I will
I learn a new turn of phrase
And it translates tenuous
Never Give Up! -I implore
And while foreign
The energy is appreciated
And I am asked to say it again

I certainly will settle in
And engage
As foreign as I am

Forces of Nature

It came in like a hurricane
Nothing left standing
Just a breeze through my fingers
In this shadow of a life
Once lived
But now living again
Nothing is stable
Nothing tied down
Nothing remains, that was
Through forces of nature
A life overturned
But to begin again
Is the freedom of happiness

Moving Away, Moving On

We gather for dinner
We gather for love
Hearts together
One last glass, a toast
We smile across the table
We smile with love
Our departure brings sadness
But also joy
We move to be happy
Our happiness infects
Smiles from all sides
One last toast
And we are gone

Tick Tock

Enveloping past madness with tears
Thinking back, speechless
The movements of a clock
The minutes become hours become days
Time, in fact, moves forward

Envelope the present with an embrace
Look around, joyful
Clocks keep ticking and ticking and ticking
In times of good or bad

Envelope the future as a dream
Yet to be had
Moisten your lips
Prepare to smile

Run

Arch your spine
Race your heart
Pump your blood
You are on the starting line
In three, two, one
You will commence your life

I was in a race that fouled
We all went back to start
I leaned in
Three, Two, One
The pistol report
Ringing in my ears
To this day
Reminds me to run
Run for my life
Run to feel alive
Because I am
Just run

Chasing False Gods

A runner, I know how to chase
Find that place where you watch the heels
ahead of you
No longer able to run, I still chase
I found the gods I had thought might help me
They did not
I was chasing false gods
Hoping for help
From a dark sky
But in the sanctuary of my love's church
I start chasing the correct God
Not exactly chasing anymore
God runs beside me
God holds my hand
I feel the warm stability of the hand of God
giving me balance
In a crooked world
Now and then, when I stumble, headed for failure
False gods fail me
But Christ holds me strong

Borrowed Steel

I'm not this strong. I'm just not.
If God hadn't loaned me a suit of armor, I would have been crushed.
I am alive because of borrowed steel

Fathering Love

That look of desire
That twist in your guts
Knotty shoulders and sweaty palms

The girl said yes
She'll arrive in spellbound grace
Her shoulders in knots

He touches her first
Hands outstretched and a thimble of fear
She leans in with apprehension

He swallows thoughts of wrong
Fathers the idea
On the muddy sidewalk, drops to his knees

Recharge

A battery of love
We need energy to give
Our very presence is an adapter
The Wi-Fi of our heart
Time apart and we are drained
Hands stretched out with desire
Fingertips miss when there is no connection
But buses and planes and the wings of our brain
Bring us home
Together, connected at last
We recharge

Timing

The timing of it all
Is breathtaking
I went from a car wreck to marrying an angel
In a blink of my brain-injured eye
To go from a squeaking wheelchair to trying to jog
To go from a memory draining like rainwater
To remembering my wedding day
To go from relearning to speak to publishing a book
In a blink, I returned to life
Kicking and screaming
In a blink, I regain consciousness
Unaware of what I was doing
To go from the deep sleep of a coma
To the wide awake smile while saying "I do"
I relearned to think
I relearned to love
My time, good people
My time has come

Acknowledgments

At 34, a nice man missed a red-light and everything about my life changed. I have a traumatic brain injury. I was a married writer about to start a new career as an English teacher. Our marriage could not survive the confusion and amnesia. When asked, I did not know I was married.

Because of the wreck, I spent close to 3 months in a coma followed by about a year in a wheelchair (I can't remember how long due to amnesia -it seemed like forever) and many more using a walker. I had 3 fractures in my pelvis, a broken clavicle, 9 sutures in my head, and five stitches in my ear. I also had 4th nerve palsy (double vision) which required surgery. Worst of all, I have a traumatic brain injury - a complex injury with a broad spectrum of symptoms and disabilities.

After more doctors and therapy than I can remember, I am a writer again with a new book coming out called Proof. I have met, fallen in love with, and married an Episcopal priest. I am not the man I once was. I am better.

It is not in spite of my suffering that I have found such happiness, it is because of my suffering that I have evolved in such a way to allow it. I may be disabled, but I am very blessed.

Acknowledgments

I would like to extend gratitude to

Spaid Rehab at UAB,

The Alabama Head Injury Foundation,

and, of course,

The Episcopal Church.

MURRAY DUNLAP is a poet, author, and artist. He received an MA in creative writing from UC Davis. In 2014 he was a finalist for the American Short Story Fiction award and is a three-time nominee for the Pushcart Prize. His work has appeared in a number of publications including *Virginia Quarterly Review*, *The Bark*, *The Pilot*, *Night Train*, and *PineStraw* magazine. He has also spent time as the Writer-in-Residence at the Weymouth Center for the Arts & Humanities in Southern Pines, North Carolina. *Bastard Blue*, his collection of short stories, was published in 2011 by Press 53. His second book, *Fires*, was published by The Ardent Writer Press in 2015. Born and raised in Mobile, Alabama, Dunlap now lives with his wife, Mary Balfour Dunlap, in Southern Pines, North Carolina.

photo credit: Jaymie Baxley

Michael Knight is the author of the novels *The Typist* and *Divining Rod*, the short story collections *Goodnight, Nobody* and *Dogfight and Other Stories*, and the book of novellas *The Holiday Season*. His most recent novel, *The Typist*, was selected as a Best Book of the Year by *The Huffington Post* and *The Kansas City Star*, among other places, and appeared on Oprah's Summer Reading List in 2011. Knight's recent collection of linked stories, *Eveningland* was the winner of the Mississippi Institute of Arts and Letters Prize in Fiction and longlisted for the 2018 Southern Book Prize. His short stories have appeared in magazines and journals like *The New Yorker, Oxford American, Paris Review* and *The Southern Review* and have been anthologized in *Best American Mystery Stories*, 2004 and *New Stories from the South: The Year's Best* 1999, 2003, 2004 and 2009. Knight teaches creative writing at the University of Tennessee and lives in Knoxville with his family.

photo credit: Judith Welch

CPSIA information can be obtained
at www.ICGtesting.com
Printed in the USA
LVHW04s1809010618
579287LV00001B/9/P